above the rim • above the rim • above the rim • above the
above the rim • above the rim • above the rim • above the rim
above the rim • above the rim • above the rim • above the rim • abo
above the rim • above the rim • above the rim • above the r
above the rim • above the rim • above the r
above the rim • above the rim • above the rim
above the rim • above the rim • above the rim • abo
above the rim • above the rim • above the rim • above the

dedicated to

all the people who live

ABOVE THE RIM

HONOR BOOKS

Above the Rim

ISBN 1-56292-850-3
Copyright © 2000 VisionQuest Communications Group, Inc.
and Koechel Peterson & Associates

HB Published by **Honor Books**
P.O. Box 55388
HONOR Tulsa, Oklahoma 74155

Research, information, and transcripts: Mary Ann Van Meter
and Annette Glavan

Text Editing: Lance Wubbels and John Humphrey

All quotes from current players are taken from interviews conducted
for various VisionQuest programs and projects.

This book in its entirety is the creation of Koechel Peterson & Associates
and VisionQuest Communications Group, Inc.

Photography by Tom Henry *(unless otherwise noted)*

Julius Erving: Andrew D. Bernstein / ALLSPORT
Michael Dickerson: Jon Ferry / ALLSPORT
Grant Hill: Jonathan Daniel / ALLSPORT
Paul Westphal: Jeff Gross / ALLSPORT
A.C. Green: Tom Hauck / ALLSPORT
Vince Carter, Kevin Garnett, Kobe Bryant: Jed Jacobson / ALLSPORT
Hersey Hawkins: Stephan Savoia / AP PHOTO
David Robinson: Al Tielemans / TIME PIX
Charlie Ward: Manny Millan / TIME PIX
Antonio McDyess: Robert Beck / TIME PIX

Be more concerned with your character than your reputation, because your character

is what you really are, while your reputation is merely what you think you are."

JOHN WOODEN

FOREWORD

When I think about playing the game *Above the Rim*, I think about a standard of excellence.

The greatest basketball players in the world play in the NBA. They make this extremely challenging sport look like the one we loved playing with our friends when we were growing up—the one we spent hour after hour practicing, all alone.

Back then we dreamed of playing the game above the rim—soaring through the air for rebounds, dunking shots, or swatting them away. We knew if we could play above the rim, we could control the game. Today's highfliers do just that, and we marvel at them.

But many players do more than achieve fantastic feats flying around the backboard, as you'll discover on the pages of this book. Several players whose exploits on the hardwood wow us are also men to be admired for their character. They not only play big, but they also stand tall as true-life champions in a world in which role models are so desperately needed.

These men have risen above the challenges of life to set a standard on the court and in society. They are magnificent athletes who consistently play the game above the rim. More than that, they demonstrate that athletic excellence need not come at the price of personal integrity. I have been privileged to cover these men over the past several years and have seen how they truly live by a higher standard.

During my playing days in the NBA, I knew I would succeed only if I maintained my game above the rim. I was blessed to do so for three years before my knees said "no more." In the aftermath of NBA glory, I discovered that playing above the rim is not nearly as important or fulfilling as living above the rim—living a life of virtue, character, and influence beyond the game.

The men who are quoted on these pages exemplify that lifestyle. They show us that through faith, courage, and determination, we, too, can strive for excellence in the games we play as well as be men and women who live above the rim. These men have been an inspiration to me. I trust they will serve you in the same manner.

CLARK KELLOGG
Basketball Analyst, CBS Sports

It is the neighborhood where the game of basketball is played, the zip code of the game's greatest players, the territory in which champions are separated from pretenders. It is where the game's greatest battles are fought, where denial and rejection take center stage, where the superstars perform air ballet, where the dunk becomes a form of art.

The game is played above the rim because a procession of supreme athletes elevated the sport to a higher level. What we see today bears little resemblance to the game created by James Naismith at a YMCA more than one hundred years ago—a slow, methodical, calculated sport of passers and set-shooters, lacking style and panache.

Elgin Baylor was the forerunner of the new era in the '50s and '60s. The wizardry of Dr. J raised the level in the '70s and '80s. And a man named Michael brought it into a whole new stratosphere in the '80s and '90s. These men spent their careers above the rim. They made the near impossible seem commonplace and forever changed the game.

Their successors—Gen-Xers such as Vince Carter, Steve Francis, and Kobe Bryant—have been charged to keep the game's present and future above the rim and to continue to set the standard for those college and high school stars who will follow in the generations to come.

Acrobats, highfliers, irresistible forces, rebounding machines—all performing wonders above the rim.

They have turned the game into an international spectacle. All around the globe, even in war-torn and poverty-stricken nations, basketball has become a phenomenon. Its terminology is an international language; its stars are worldwide celebrities; and its exploits are dreams for young men and women of all cultures. On every continent, young people long to play the game above the rim.

Above the rim is where the greatest challenges occur. It is here that the ball is up for grabs, available for the taking. Those who take command above the rim take charge of the game itself. To take control above the rim is to own prime roundball real estate.

Above the rim is where moments in time become suspended in history, where improvisations become enduring snapshots, where the improbable becomes legendary.

"There's a feeling of power that's awesome
when you're up in the air and over the rim.
There's not too much like that."

DAVID ROBINSON

of the moment.

Legendary plays are made above the rim.

These are the moments that have made us shake our heads in disbelief, wondering how a human being could have done it. Kareem's sky hook with three defenders draped on him. Magic's baby hook over a seven-footer. Bird's tip-in while being knocked to the floor. The Admiral coming from the free-throw line with an "outta' my way" expression for a follow-up jam. Tim

If somebody asks, 'Are you watching the game tonight?' you know what game they're talking about. They are talking about your game because it's the only game going."

KEVIN JOHNSON

Duncan's expressionless, authoritative rejection that sends the ball to a seat in the third row. Shaq's explosive dunk that changes the address of the basket itself. Vince Carter's breakaway, 360-degree tomahawk slam. Dr. J's twirling scoop shot from behind, around, and under the backboard. Jordan, seemingly suspended in midair—twisting, hanging, evading, while laying it in. All scenes that will undoubtedly wind up someday in an NBA time capsule.

Legendary players play above the rim.

They wow us. They draw us to watch the game, waiting for what they will do next. The future of the game is carved in their image. Basketball, more than any other sport, is a game of superstars—men who clearly stand above their peers and can single-handedly take control of a game, a week, a series, or a season. Garnett. Iverson. Carter. Kobe. Shaq. Duncan. Hill. These men see the game as their stage, the ball as their friend, and the atmosphere above the rim as their territory. They have made basketball a vehicle to shape the twenty-first-century culture by building their reputations above the rim.

Legendary people live above the rim.

The game's real heroes build their lives above the rim. They are compelled not only to stake their reputations on their exploits in the "air up there" but also to build their lives on what lies beyond the game and well above the rim.

"I think the game has to be fun. It was meant to be fun. Everybody started playing the game because it was fun. That doesn't mean there aren't hard aspects of it, because there certainly are. But if you play feeling worried or angry, you're not going to be as effective as when you're free and loose."

PAUL WESTPHAL

"You have to be dedicated. You have to be teachable, to want to grow. Each year you always want to improve upon what you did the season before. I've never been content with what I've done in the past."

ARMEN GILLIAM

These hoop heroes are men who have overcome adversity, silenced doubters, faithfully shown up for work every day, and become examples of virtue. They are not fazed by volatile fans, not swayed by critical media, and not sidetracked by a poor performance. They live above their mistakes and failures, above trades, injuries, and salary cuts. They know their roles and are content to excel in those alone. Passers, shooters, defensive stoppers, shot blockers, rebounders, sixth men, or role players—they take their skill, mix in passion and determination, and elevate their game and that of those around them.

They serve as inspirations. They play for the love of the game and to influence others. They desire to shape culture by the way they play and the way they live—above the rim.

"We wouldn't be in this game, and we wouldn't be doing what we're doing, if we didn't want to compete. We want to win. I'm not here to be passive, to sit back and watch somebody do whatever he wants. This is my career, and I want to be the best in it. I know the game is going to go to the aggressive player, and it's going to go to the aggressive team. I want us to go out there and win the game."

A. C. GREEN

"There's only one guy who's going to put the crown on or put the ring on. I have to play like I'm the one who's going to get that ring."

DAVID ROBINSON

"The biggest thing is how a person goes about winning. It's about sportsmanship, how we win. Being a champion takes determination and the will to endure the rough times. If you can endure those tough times, you'll come out on top."

CHARLIE WARD

"The heart of a champion belongs to a person who can sacrifice, who can lead a team. There have to be sacrifices made on and off the court to be a champion. You have to be a leader. Everyone who plays the game is a part of a family. Being the point guard on the team is like being a father. You're the point guard of that family. So, it's all about sacrifice."

CHRIS CHILDS

POINT GUARDS

They are basketball's little big men. While most of them play the game below the rim, they elevate the game of others. Their goal is to inspire those around them to greatness, constantly pushing teammates to play above the rim.

They have nicknames like Tiny, The Skate, Mugsy, and Spud. They are real-life versions of *The Little Train That Could.* Yet it's not physical size that matters here. Rather, it's the size of heart, depth of desire, and expanse of will that count.

A point guard is the team's quarterback. He directs the offense, calls the plays. Like a general leading his troops into battle in a hostile environment, when confidence wanes, all look to him. As he responds to the circumstances, so do his comrades.

"Being a point guard in the NBA, you must know the strengths and weaknesses of your personnel as well as every player on the opposing team. You must know all the offensive and defensive sets. You can't just look at the man you are guarding that night. You must know everything that's happening on the court at all times. You must be involved in all the preparation phases of the game, so you can be on top of your game when you step on the court."

AVERY JOHNSON

"Being a point guard, if I'm not scoring, I have to do other thin[gs] on the court to help my team win. Whether it's to distribute the ball to guy[s] who are in a position to score, or to pick up the level of our defensive intensi[ty] by picking up full court or getting a steal, I always have to be able to [do] something more. So I'm not going to let statistics dictate how I pla[y]."

KEVIN JOHNSO[N]

He is like a maestro of the hardwood, conducting a basketball symphony. When he has all sections in harmony, not a note is missed, scoring comes in crescendos, and the crowd stands in approval.

The point guard is an extension of the coach on the floor. He must see the game developing before him—both on offense and defense. He must run the break under control, but fast. He must get the ball to the big men inside, but also be able to hit the long jumper. He must penetrate the lane and fearlessly attack the opposing defense. He must make split-second decisions—pass, shoot, or take it to the hoop. He must be able to get back on defense to stop a break on the other end and have the anticipation to break up a two-on-one. He is the one who must keep the rest of his team in the game mentally, knowing whom to bark at one minute and whom to pat on the back the next.

"It's like poetry ... pure perfection. It's the most beautiful thing you can imagine ... like an orchestra. It's incredible to direct the show, put the ball in the right hands, keep it from guys, be a leader, set the example, and be the extension of the coach on the floor. It's a great feeling. You're in total control."

POINT GUARDS

PASSING FANCY

A point guard is an adept passer who can really "dish the rock." He is a "dime-dropper." Most of the time this is what he does best, and he can do so in the tightest of spaces, with or without looking.

Most have been moved to point guard at some juncture because they were too small or couldn't shoot well enough to play anywhere else. Many of them have made it through on court smarts and sheer determination. When the team is playing poorly, they are usually the first to come under fire, finding themselves unappreciated, traded, or cut.

The point guard carries a tremendous load on his almost-always undersized shoulders. His makeup must provide for an iron will, a joyful exuberance, steely nerves, and an ability to weather criticism.

Yet, it is a position that none of these men would trade for any other.

"I want to create and put the ball in the right hands. I want to be able to make the right decisions because I've prepared night in and night out. I want the rock in my hands. You can create something special. You can make something happen. You are the decision maker."

"To make a perfectly placed pass to one of my teammates who knocks down the shot, that what it's all about. It's an unselfish act that's simply pure basketball, and it wins games. When I make a key shot, I get excited, but if I can put the ball in the right hands and that guy knocks down a shot, our entire team is thrilled. It becomes contagious."

"People may think that that was pure reaction, but in reality it was a reaction I've practiced a thousand times."

MARK JACKSON

POINT GUARDS

"On a fast break, you have to see your players on the wings and know whether they can take a couple of dribbles to finish or just catch and lay it up. You have to know what the defense is doing and what you can do to get an easy shot for the team. In a split second you have to recognize the situation and make the right play."

TYUS EDNEY

FAST BREAK

It looks like controlled chaos. Five men run down the court at breakneck speed, all trying to get into position to make something great happen. Five other men race down the court equally as fast, trying to stop that something great from happening.

The fast break is one of the game's superlative forms of entertainment. Anything can happen . . . and usually does. Two-on-one, three-on-two, three-on-one—it's a defender's nightmare.

Running the break well takes a special skill. You have to anticipate the defenders, spot the men filling the lanes and the trailer, fake, look away, read, and react . . . in the blink of an eye.

"Throughout my years as an athlete, I've learned that if you give 100 percent during a game and you make mistakes, then you can blame yourself. But if you give 100 percent and you lose, you can't ask for anything more. People make a big deal of losing and winning. It is a big deal, but if you give your all and do the things you are capable of doing, then you don't have to worry about winning and losing. Those things will take care of themselves."

CHARLIE WARD

"Bringing the ball down the middle of the floor and baiting and playing the defenders like an accordion, that is a dream. When you come down on a break with guys who can fly from anywhere and finish, it's almost like a game of cat and mouse."

MARK JACKSON

But as the tempo rises, so does the risk. What should be a dunk, a layup, or an uncontested jumper can easily turn into a dropped pass, a kicked ball, or an offensive foul. The risk-reward factor is high. A great fast break can turn the game's momentum and kick the offense into high gear.

Teams that run it to precision surgically cut defenders to pieces. The Lakers dominated the league and won championships in the '80s with the break. Now, teams must run in order to win. The up-tempo game is in. Up the tempo, and you up the emotion.

"God has given me the ability to score almost at will at times, and there are times for that. But that's not what it's all about. The most satisfaction I get out of playing basketball is to get my teammates involved and see them finish off a play. I love to see them excited and help them feel like they are making a major contribution."

KEVIN JOHNSON

"I get this question all the time. 'What do I need to become a good shooter?' My answer is to say, 'About six hours a day.'"

MARK PRICE

SHOOTERS

The game's great shooters are like men who live in their own world.

When they are on, it seems as though they are throwing peas into the ocean. For the great ones, the hoop looks bigger and bigger and the ball smaller and more in their control. Everything around them is silenced out—the crowd, the music, and defenders. They have laser lock on the bottom of the net and tunnel vision to the front of the rim. Range is not an issue when they are "in the zone." It's an address only the few in this small fraternity know. They've been there before.

"I think everyone can be a really good shooter if they practice, work on repetition, and continue to want to improve. But I think I have a gift to be able to shoot the ball. When I was growing up, I don't remember shooting for hours, looking at the mechanics, and trying to do the fundamentals in shooting. It just came very, very naturally to me."

HUBERT DAVIS

Shooters who are in the zone can completely turn the momentum of a game. Nothing takes the opposing crowd out of a game or brings the home crowd and his teammates back into it like a mad bomber draining three-pointers from way downtown. The farther out he goes, the lower his opponent sinks, soon becoming completely demoralized and eventually being taken out of the game.

Great shooters will shoot anytime, anywhere, and in any situation. Fall-away, running one-hander, pull-up jumper—any type of shot from any spot on the floor. Double-teamed, triple-teamed, it doesn't matter when they're on fire. If a defender relaxes for a split second, it's over. All they need is someone to get the ball to them.

"I'm a coach's son, and we just lived in the gym a lot when we were young. Going in by ourselves and shooting, day after day—that's the one way to get good. I still love watching the ball go in."

BRYCE DREW

If they do hit a cold streak, they just keep shooting until they get hot again. Miss 8 in a row, keep throwing it up. Soon 0 for 7 turns into 12 for 20. Ready, aim, fire!

Jerry West, Pete Maravich, Mark Price, Larry Bird, Michael Jordan—these men wanted to have the ball in their hands with the game on the line. So did their teammates, their fans, and their coaches. It was as close to a sure thing as there was in the game.

Some of today's sharpshooters include Hubert Davis, Glen Rice, Allan Houston, and Reggie Miller. They are feared, deadly, and the focus of every defensive game plan. Try to shut them down, and they become even more competitive.

Are great shooters born or made? Both. It's a combination of God-given talent and spending hour upon hour at the gym, shooting thousands of shots, perfecting the form. Flick the wrist, fingertip release, rotation, follow-through, arc, spin . . . *nothing but net.*

"It's hard work, preparing yourself, and requires a lot of discipline. When I miss two, three, four shots, sometimes I tend to not want to shoot a three-pointer anymore. But being a shooter, you have to be mentally strong. You have to shoot even when you're missing shots. You have to stay mentally strong and keep shooting it."

MICHAEL DICKERSON

"I just go out there and play, and let the basketball do the talking."

HERSEY HAWKINS

"When you have confidence in what you're doing and know you're a good shooter, you really believe your next shot is going in."

MARK PRICE

"Just keep shooting. When you're a shooter, that's what defines you. You keep shooting, feeling the percentages are in your favor because you know how well you can shoot."

BRENT PRICE

BIG MEN

BIG MEN

The men in the middle. They are Twin Towers, Skyscrapers, Wilt the Stilt, Big E, and Shaq Attack.

The game has evolved into a battle of seven-footers who challenge one another for real estate in and around the paint. Two hundred-fifty-pound bodies bang for territory. They lean on, grab, elbow, shove, bump, back in, muscle, pound, and push one another. Always jockeying for position, always trying to gain an advantage, they play without padding or protection.

The men in the middle are intimidators. They claim the territory in the paint. Smaller trespassers receive a menacing glare, clearly a warning that it is not wise to come into their territory.

Some big men are scorers; others are primarily rebounders and a defensive presence, and a few do it all. No matter what game they bring, they are always in for a physical battle.

Mikan. Russell. Chamberlain. Jabbar. Olajuwan. Robinson. Shaq. There have been few truly dominant centers in basketball history—men who had teams built entirely around them and who turned their teams into champions.

"Basketball is a very physical sport inside the paint.

My job is to clog up the paint, make myself big,

make myself a physical player,

and always be willing to give contact."

ANDREW LANG

"*Every team and every game features a talented big man, and some teams have the great centers. Every night you face quality players. When you step on the court, you take on a different persona. That doesn't mean you get arrogant and curse the officials and go crazy. It means that off the court you are nice and friendly to everyone, but when you get on the court, you are going to play tough and hard and aggressive.*"

TODD FULLER

DAVID ROBIN

"When you go out on the floor, people have an expectation of you to perform, and you have to perform to a certain level. I also feel a responsibility to God to perform at a certain level as a husband and father. Those are things that take an investment of time. On the court, I have to go and spend time in the gym, shooting and lifting weights to prepare myself. At home, I have to spend time investing in my children and in my wife. My worth as a person comes from what I do for God and being able to go to God and say, 'God, are You proud of me? I'm doing what You called me to do.' That's where my self-worth comes from. It comes from pleasing Him."

"It's very physical. There are big bodies out there all the time. It makes it very tough mentally and physically because you know you can't go out there and have a mediocre night. So you have to be tough-minded and tough physically. Physically, because you have three-hundred-pound guys banging on you, and mentally, because the pressure is there every night to perform."

ISON

"The thing that keeps driving me is that I don't have to trust in what I can do. I have to trust in what God can do. What God does is real special. It always exceeds what you think."

"The fans are great, and you get a lot of energy from them, but that's not what drives me as an athlete. What drives me is the challenge of being great every night. What drives me every night for eight months of the season is another opportunity to go out there and do something special."

"I developed a heart problem and ended up having three surgeries to correct it. When I was lying on the operating table, I gave my life over to God. I just said, 'Lord, You're in control. I can't control what's going to happen here.' Ever since then I've been following His lead."
BRYCE DREW

"I deal with adversity through prayer— that's the only way. I have to sometimes sit back, analyze the situation, then I have to pray about it. There's been a lot of adversities in my career. I spent nine years on losing teams and had a lot of uphill battles. Now I sit back and learn what to pray for real quick."
WAYMAN TISDALE

HALFTIME

Halftime can be a brutal time for a basketball player. If his team is up and he's got a hot hand, he doesn't want to take a break and risk cooling down. If his team is down, he'll likely spend most of the fifteen minutes being chewed out by an ornery coach. Either way, he'd rather stay out on the court.

Adversity comes to every player—bad games, bad shots, bad choices.

But halftime also provides an opportunity to look within, to create new strategies and change assignments. At halftime, the self-directed questions are asked about what you're really made of. What do you have to draw upon for the second half? Will you fold under the pressure or turn it up a notch?

It's an opportunity to reenergize and refocus. It's a time to set your sights on what is ahead, what can be, not what has been. You can get back in the game.

"I suffered my first knee injury right before my third year in the league. God allows things to happen sometimes for a reason, and sometimes we get an opportunity to understand what the reason was. I feel that any questions I have about His plan for my life, especially as I look back on how He's brought me through injury after injury, who am I to question Him and His plan?"

LAPHONSO ELLIS

"A champion is not always going to be somebody who wins every game or wins every battle or makes the right decisions all the time. But I think a champion is somebody who can deal with the tough times, and he can deal with them well. There are going to be good times for everybody. But it's how you come through the bad times that tells if you're a champion or not."

SEAN ELLIOTT

"The game of basketball is won and lost in the paint. No matter what position you play, you have to be able to play in the paint to win a basketball game."

RONNIE GRANDISON

IN THE PAINT

Life in the paint is like being stuck in rush-hour traffic between convoys of semis. Clogged with big bodies, no room to maneuver, and formidable obstacles to get around, the paint can be rugged. Big men banging on one another within a confined area can be a bit like powder kegs near flames. Intensity can create a spark.

"The big guys are going to bump and pound you a little bit—that's just part of my game. I wish I was a better perimeter shooter at times, so I could shoot around from the outside. But my team needs me to penetrate, to get in the paint and draw fouls, so I have to do it. I got a few bumps and bruises along the way to show for it."

KEVIN JOHNSON

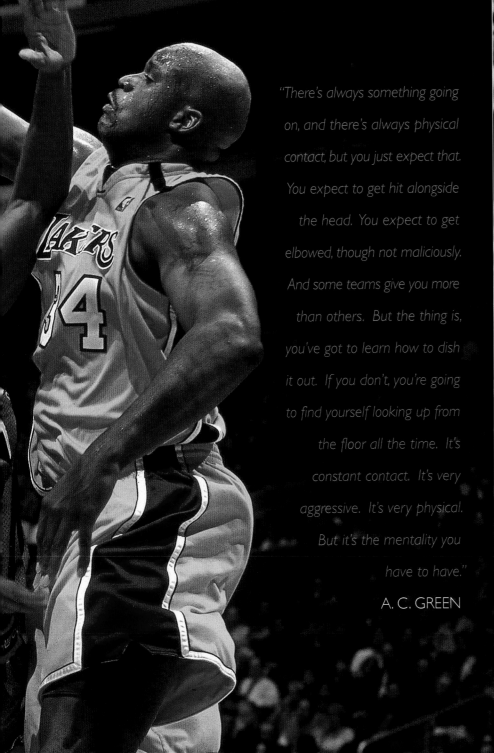

"There's always something going on, and there's always physical contact, but you just expect that. You expect to get hit alongside the head. You expect to get elbowed, though not maliciously. And some teams give you more than others. But the thing is, you've got to learn how to dish it out. If you don't, you're going to find yourself looking up from the floor all the time. It's constant contact. It's very aggressive. It's very physical. But it's the mentality you have to have."

A. C. GREEN

But what takes place in the paint creates some of the game's most exciting moments—high-wire battles for rebounds, off-balance tip-ins, reverse lay-ups, in-your-face dunks.

Those who play in the paint pick their spots carefully and attack. Some of the game's great scorers make a living here. Tim Duncan. Kevin Garnett. Shaq. Vin Baker.

They use leverage and positioning, head fakes and quickness, baseline drives and power moves, drop steps and pivots, short jump shots and soft fadeaways. Most often they play with their backs to the basket, always staying aware of where they are. They post up and back in.

Defense here is an act of will. Do not give ground and do not leave the baseline unprotected. If you lose the battle in the paint, you lose the war.

"The big guys say, 'This is my paint.' It's just fun to go in there and lay it up over them. They swipe at the ball and miss. That's a thrill. I laid one up over Mutombo one time, and he looked at me like he was saying, 'Don't you watch cable?' So it was fun to go and just lay it up right up over him."

TYUS EDNEY

REJECTION

REJECTION

What does it feel like to put up a shot and see it come back your way at twice the velocity? Or see it wind up in the lap of a guy in the third row, between his popcorn and soda?

Shot blockers are intimidators. They strike fear in an opponent. Shot blockers make shooters alter their shots and think twice about shooting again. Break a shooter's confidence even a crack, and you've succeeded.

Rejection is the antidote to the dunk. Reject, and you turn the momentum, initiating fear. Rejection is power.

"My job is to be intimidating,

to block shots, to rebound,

and to be a force defensively.

I have to stop people inside the paint."

ANDREW LANG

"We're not friends on the court. I'm not friends with

anybody on the court. As a matter of fact, I don't even

like guys on the court. You have to understand, it's your

team against their team. If Michael Jordan comes soaring

through the air, it's my job to hit him. It's my job to make

sure he's not going to score when he comes through.

It's him or me, and only one of us can survive."

DAVID ROBINSON

"Concentrate on going up strong and trying to put the ball in the basket. You have to be able to explode to the basket or David Robinson will squash you like a grape."

RONNIE GRANDISON

TAKE IT
TO THE HOOP

Taking it to the hoop is what creates defining moments in a player's career. One play can produce a memory that towers above the rest, a highlight-reel play forever etched in the scrapbook of our minds.

Crossover dribble, head fake, shake your man, take it fearlessly into the land of the giants guarding the hoop. With a lightning-quick first step, he's by his man and on his way to the rack where he either scores, is sent to the free-throw line, or even worse, does both. With every action, he seems to say, "Get out of my way or pay the price."

Go all the way for the slam, lay it in, bank it in off the glass, or stop and put up a baby jumper. Whatever you do, take it in hard and take it in strong. And don't be intimidated. You'll survive to come calling again another day.

"In the NBA you have to be able to go by people and take it to the basket. If you jab step and he doesn't react, you can go right by him. Then if you jab and he reacts, you can pump fake the shot and go to the basket."

HUBERT DAVIS

"When I'm playing basketball, it's David versus Goliath.

I feel the big guys have a huge advantage on me in certain

areas, but in other areas I have the advantage. They claim

the paint as their turf, and I feel my duty is to trespass as

often as I can. And there's nothing more exhilarating

for a little guy than to dunk on a big guy."

KEVIN JOHNSON

DEFENSE

DEFENSE

Man-to-man. Trap. Switch. Press. Match-up. Weak-side help. Put a hand in his face. Move your feet. Anticipate. Don't give up the baseline.

In a game dominated by renowned offensive players and spectacular offensive plays, the game is still won by a strong defense. From Russell to Jordan, the game's greatest players have always been tenacious on both ends of the court. They knew that stopping their opponent was as important as putting the rock in the hoop.

"If I want to be out there on the floor and compete, which is what I love to do, then I have to play defense. So this is the role I can provide for this team, and that's giving tough defensive presence in the back court. That's what I thrive on."

BRYANT STITH

"I'm a big shot blocker, and if they don't give me the ball

I can still make things happen on the defensive end.

can block shots, make steals, and make other things

happen. Blocking a shot is great, especially on someone

you know or someone who's been talking trash

DAVID ROBINSON

"I think I can speak on behalf of most

big guys. When a little guy comes in

the lane and tries to lay it up, you want

to make him feel sorry that he did that."

TODD FULLER

One has to want to be a great defensive player to become one. Playing defense is as thankless as manning the offensive line in football. It is a grind-it-out, sacrificial style of play that values hustle over recognition. Working at it is ignominy; succeeding is anonymity. But true greatness on defense—to literally shut down the league's premier scorers, night in and night out—is incredibly fulfilling.

Make no mistake, great teams play great defense. The '60s Celtics had Russell and Jones. The '70s Celtics had Havlicek and Chaney, while the Lakers had West and Chamberlain. In the '80s, the Sixers had Bobby Jones and Moses Malone; L.A. featured Kareem and Michael Cooper; Boston had Kevin McHale and Dennis Johnson. The '90s saw Chicago with Jordan and Pippen.

On every level, defense wins games and championships.

"When you dunk on somebody, that's got to be the best feeling. There is nothing like dunking. My first couple of years in the league, when I went up and somebody tried to block it, I would dunk as hard as I could. I growled because it was such an awesome feeling. Now I don't really growl so much, but, you know, when somebody's been dunked on, they know it. People say that a dunk is only two points, but a dunk is more than two points—it's two points plus some intimidation."

DAVID ROBINSON

SCORERS

SCORERS

If you're having a good shooting night, it's like magic. The rim is as big as an ocean. throw it up there and, even if you close your eyes, it's going to go in. When I'm having a good g I especially want the rock. Nobody can stop me. At money time, having the rock when time elapsed and the score is tied and you are shooting two free throws, that's when I wa

TOM HAMMON

"I've proven myself in this league. And I think I've had a pretty good career. So, sometimes you're not going to be one of the media favorites. I'm not so worried about that recognition."

SEAN ELLIOTT

Their names are on the marquees. Their faces adorn the covers of media guides. Their every action is detailed by beat writers. These are the men whom opposing coaches lose hair over trying to figure out how to stop. They are the ones whom people pay hundreds of dollars each night to sit at courtside and be mesmerized by.

Jordan. West. Robertson. Bird. Frazier. Magic. Malone. Garnett. Maravich.

They are small forwards or big guards . . . or sometimes both. They can single-handedly dominate a game and often embarrass defenders.

Scorers find ways to get points. If they are shooting poorly from outside, they will take the ball to the hoop. They work for their shots, move well away from the ball, know how to rub their man off a pick, and are experts at setting up a defender.

"It's whatever the defense gives you. If you get the ball on the perimeter, and the guy is right there and he's not on you, you take the shot."

HUBERT DAVIS

scorers

BLUE-COLLAR WORKERS

Basketball's blue-collar workers are rare individuals. In today's game of "look at me," these men are content to fill a role that never puts them on the front page or in the highlight reels.

They are big, rugged, dedicated men, whose play is marked by a fierce intensity. It's as if they bring a lunch pail and hard hat to the arena every night. They scrap on the boards, draw the charge, set the screens, box out in the key, and play "in your face" defense. They do all the tough things that don't show up in the box score.

A typical line for them in the box score reads: 38 minutes played, 3 points, 1-2 field goals, 1-1 free throws, 11 rebounds, 4 personal fouls, 0 turnovers. And they are perfectly content with this.

"If I'm playing against a center who's a real banger, it's going to be a physical confrontation. I usually give up a lot of weight and size to a guy like that. So, I have to prepare myself mentally and physically to go out there and compete every night."

ARMON GILLIAM

They are counted on to grab rebounds, defend the opponent's top scorer, make key passes, set bone-jarring picks, and do all the intangible things that help a team win. While the scorers take a limousine to the game, these guys call a cab.

They pride themselves on being there, ready to play every night. Hangnails won't stop them, neither will strains, sprains, stitches, bruises, black eyes, nor missing teeth.

Blue-collar men are underrated and too often under-appreciated. Yet they are all for the team. Without them, victory is impossible.

They are all grit and no glamour, yet they are invaluable.

"There is definitely a physical toll, but I'm a very physical person. I protect the lane and my teammates. I have the reputation of being the enforcer on the team. My motto is that you have to get them before they get you. It's a dog-eat-dog world in there."

TOM HAMMONDS

"God has given me the challenge every single day to do the best I can and to do it consistently. I wake up in the morning and don't want to go to practice. I can call in sick or take two vacation days if I want. But that's not me, and that's not how I play or prepare for the game. There's something within me that drives and motivates me to get there to that game, to that practice, and not only to get to it, but through it."

"It's very, very simple to be mediocre, to do nothing, to just be normal—no opinions, no ideas, no convictions, just living to be living. This is my mission field. This is where God has placed me. I'm trying to get inside these guys' lives and challenge them in the hard areas and say to them, 'Look, rise up and be a man. It's easy to be a male, but be a man. Stand up for what you know you should be doing.' "

A.C. GREEN

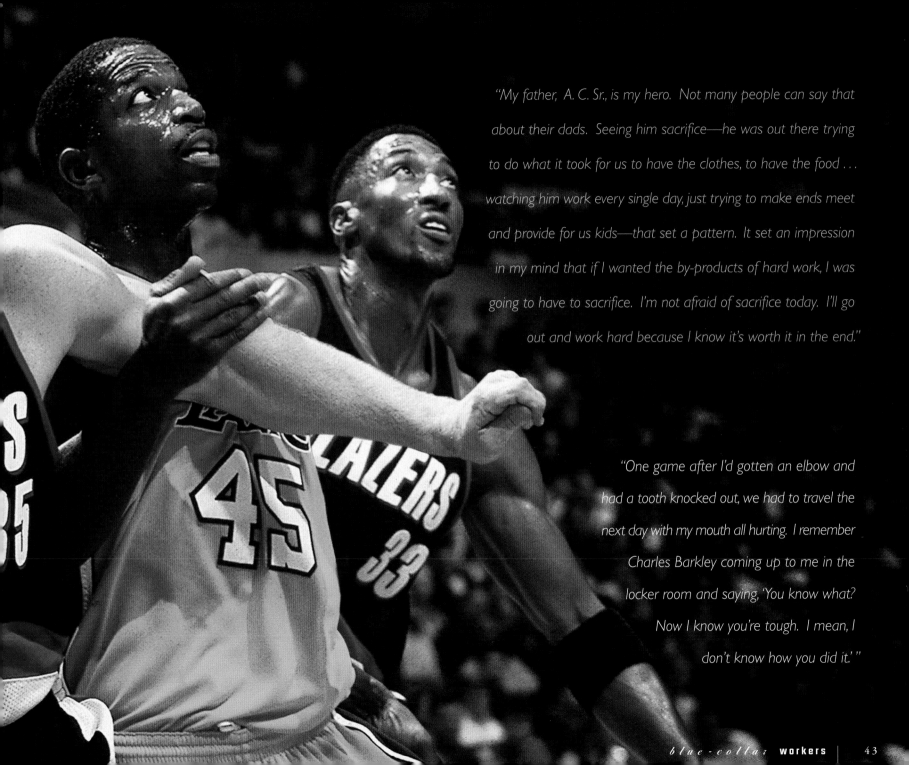

"My father, A. C. Sr., is my hero. Not many people can say that about their dads. Seeing him sacrifice—he was out there trying to do what it took for us to have the clothes, to have the food … watching him work every single day, just trying to make ends meet and provide for us kids—that set a pattern. It set an impression in my mind that if I wanted the by-products of hard work, I was going to have to sacrifice. I'm not afraid of sacrifice today. I'll go out and work hard because I know it's worth it in the end."

"One game after I'd gotten an elbow and had a tooth knocked out, we had to travel the next day with my mouth all hurting. I remember Charles Barkley coming up to me in the locker room and saying, 'You know what? Now I know you're tough. I mean, I don't know how you did it.'"

COACHES

COACHES

I think that having been a player, I understand what players are going through. I want to bring out their strengths and hide their weaknesses. That's what coaches are supposed to do."

PAUL WESTPHAL

Basketball coaches are chronic sufferers. Some bite towels, throw clipboards, kick water coolers, scold players, yell at referees, and chew antacids. Many are volcanic eruptions waiting to happen.

Like a man seated on a roller coaster ride that never ends, a basketball coach must weather ups and downs and emotional twists and turns that are constant. Watching a coach throughout the course of a close game can make an onlooker exhausted.

The best of the coaches is a master psychologist, taskmaster, inventor, counselor, public speaker, policeman, mad scientist, father figure, strategist, promoter, friend, and motivator . . . all rolled into one body. And while he performs the nearly impossible task of juggling the roles, he is required to keep his Armani suit sweat-free.

"Sometimes, it's just misery. Other times you feel like you're just stealing because it's so easy and fun. You don't want to derive your identity from what happens. When things are going good, it's easy to believe all the good things and think you're better than you are. When things are going bad, people beat you down and you end up thinking you're just low as can be. In reality, the truth is probably somewhere in-between. So don't ride the roller coaster and believe it."

PAUL WESTPHAL

A COACH MUST KNOW HOW TO:

- adjust to new players and injuries.

- encourage and discipline every player on his team.

- play the crowd and work the officials.

- put the right player combination on the floor every night.

- play to his team's strengths and his opponents' weaknesses.

- find the proper team chemistry and create an atmosphere within which to build a winner.

- develop a nineteen-year-old with a tender psyche, while also encouraging a wily veteran.

- handle the ego of a superstar, yet not let the last man on the bench get lost.

"As important as it is, and as all-consuming

as it is, I remember that it's just basketball.

You compete as hard as you can, and then the

game's over and you move on to the next game.

It's important to keep it in perspective. You give

everything you have to it, but it's not real life."

PAUL WESTPHAL

Building and then managing a team is a challenge. It is said that basketball is a players' game, but that seems shortsighted. Would the great teams of the recent era have been as successful with another man at the helm? The Lakers flourished under Pat Riley's flair for an open style and masterful motivation. The Bad Boy Pistons needed the patience and direction of Chuck Daly. Houston required the calm strength of Rudy Tomjanovich. And Phil Jackson gave the Bulls the structure in which to succeed. With so many competitive teams and so many talented players, today's coach must give his million-dollar players an edge.

"I have a sign on my desk that says, 'It takes eighteen years of hard work to be an overnight success.' I was behind the scenes and had a lot of opportunities and a lot of people who opened doors for me. I feel very fortunate to be in the position I'm in now."

RANDY PFUND

> *"I respect where my players are. I'm there for them when their babies are delivered and when they have knee surgery. I'm there if they are having marital or family troubles. I'm more than a coach to my players, because if you give yourself to me, the least I can do is give myself to you."*

JOHN LUCAS

Changes in the game and its surroundings have brought changes to the men who hope to shape it. With increased complexity and pressures, perhaps a coach's greatest attribute is adaptability. He can no longer install a system and mold players around it. Rather, he must look at his personnel and choose a system that best suits them. Today, a coach must be a people person who is more intent on gaining respect than obedience. His biggest challenge is keeping players interested in basketball rather than in the swirl of off-the-court distractions.

Coaches today must be able to relate to their players. The "old school"—Xs and Os and discipline—is out. "Communication" is in. Coaches are like chess players. Every move is calculated. A benching, a hug, a key substitution, a technical foul—all play a role in the present game, and perhaps in the next game, and possibly even those two or three years down the road.

But to get down the road, the coach must win now. Playing for today with an eye on tomorrow is paramount. If not, he'll soon be looking for a new job.

> *"On every team, you have some good people. You also have some swinging people who will be to the good side if the good have control and to the bad side if the bad have control. And then you have the rotten apples in every organization."*

DAN ISSEL

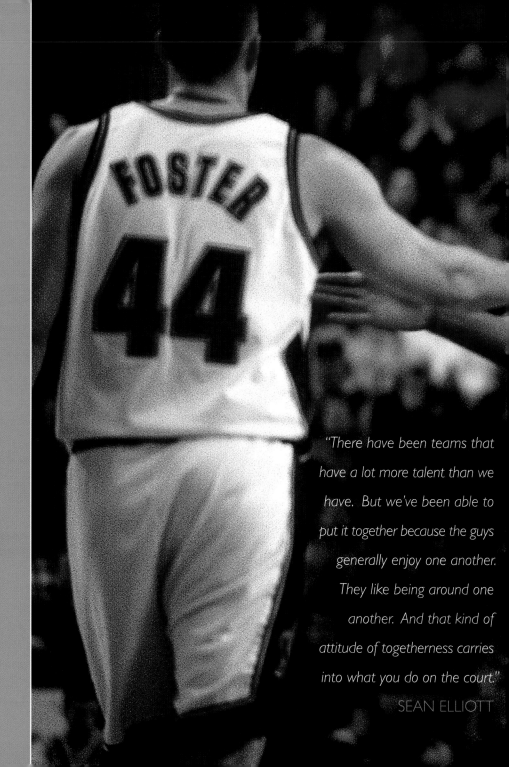

TEAM
TEAMWORK

Pick and roll. Give and go. Backdoor cut. Switch on defense. Double team. Trap. The best teams work together. Stockton and Malone. Robinson and Duncan. Hardaway and Mourning. But it's more than the big two. When the shooter is cold or the big man fouls out, someone else has to step up. Every winning team has a defensive stopper, a rebounder, and a passer/penetrator to complement the inside and outside scorers. Winning is a habit created when various individual parts function together for the good of the whole.

Teamwork is about diversity within unity. Each player on the roster fills an important role. After the starting five, most teams bring three or four key men off the bench, without whom they cannot consistently win. The sixth man can often be a team's most valuable player, counted on to score and defend. Numbers seven and eight bang the boards and provide a perimeter shooting threat. Number nine runs the point for a few minutes to give the starter a breather.

"There have been teams that have a lot more talent than we have. But we've been able to put it together because the guys generally enjoy one another. They like being around one another. And that kind of attitude of togetherness carries into what you do on the court."

SEAN ELLIOTT

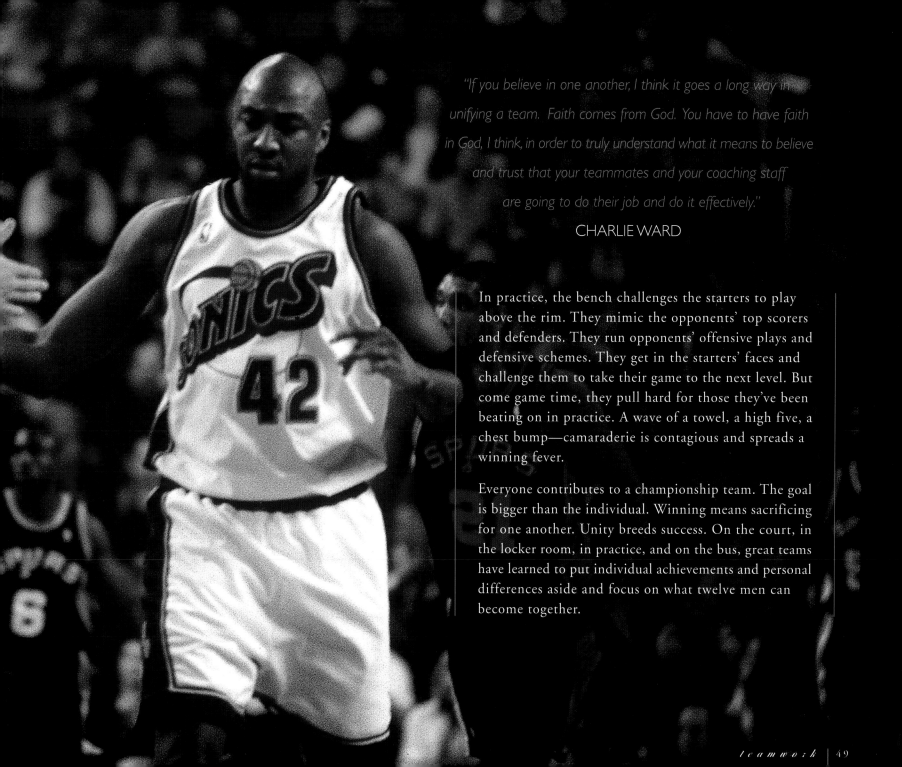

"If you believe in one another, I think it goes a long way in unifying a team. Faith comes from God. You have to have faith in God, I think, in order to truly understand what it means to believe and trust that your teammates and your coaching staff are going to do their job and do it effectively."

CHARLIE WARD

In practice, the bench challenges the starters to play above the rim. They mimic the opponents' top scorers and defenders. They run opponents' offensive plays and defensive schemes. They get in the starters' faces and challenge them to take their game to the next level. But come game time, they pull hard for those they've been beating on in practice. A wave of a towel, a high five, a chest bump—camaraderie is contagious and spreads a winning fever.

Everyone contributes to a championship team. The goal is bigger than the individual. Winning means sacrificing for one another. Unity breeds success. On the court, in the locker room, in practice, and on the bus, great teams have learned to put individual achievements and personal differences aside and focus on what twelve men can become together.

CHALK TALK

Coaches strategize and motivate. Players perform and sometimes fail. Teams win and lose.

Basketball is as much like life as it is a game. Success and failure go hand in hand. An apparent victory can be reversed in a matter of seconds by the unusual bounce of a ball. On occasion, shots seemingly all the way in the hoop inexplicably pop out. The man with the hot hand one night can't get anything to fall on the next. A furious comeback is halted when time simply runs out.

This game, like life, is filled with surprises, opportunities, exhilaration, and crushing disappointments. But there is always the next game, the next pass, the next shot. A chance for redemption always comes.

Plays are diagrammed for success. Players must have faith in the system and listen to the coach, and their opportunity will come. If they persevere, they will have a day to play above the rim.

LAPHONSO ELLIS

To live above the rim requires a strategy as well. The diagram from the chalkboard of life comes from the ultimate "Coach." His strategy is proven for lasting success. In this "game," some are scorers, some set picks, some defend, and some rebound. But all are in the game, playing under a Coach who takes pleasure in motivating them to live at the highest level and play for the sheer joy the game brings.

Playing above the rim means playing to a higher standard. Playing to a higher standard means playing for an audience of one. And so it is in the heart of a champion. A true champion doesn't want someone else controlling his destiny. He wants the ball in his hands at this game's end, to follow the winning strategy, and to hear the Coach say, "Well done!"

"Winning was the ultimate. I had a passion, a love, a desire, a dedication to be the best and to win. When I gave my life to Christ, it only put everything in perspective and put it into a shell around the greatest champion of them all, Jesus Christ, the one whom I live for and whom I serve."

MARK JACKSON

POST GAME

"If you're a Christian, it doesn't mean you'll always have all the money you need. It doesn't mean you'll have perfect health or life without problems. But it does mean that the Lord will give you a peace that will make sure you can survive anything."

DAN ISSEL

"The bottom line is that I'm a servant of God. Whomever I come in contact with, it's up to me whether I make their day a little brighter or more pleasant. I don't have all the answers, but if I can let my light shine in a godly way through what I say, how I act, or how I approach them, I think it makes a difference."

HERSEY HAWKINS

"I wouldn't trade my relationship with the Lord for fame, for glamour, for being the Michael Jordan of the NBA, or anything else. Knowing Him is much more important than any of that."

BRYCE DREW

"It was my second year in the league, and I thought I had everything. Then all of a sudden, I realized God had given me everything. But never once had I stopped and said, 'Thank You, God, for giving me all I have.' That day I just cried out and said, 'Lord, I am so sorry. I didn't realize I was being a spoiled brat. Thank You for everything You've given me. You blessed me beyond comprehension. Everything I have I want to give back to You.' And, man, He turned my life around 180 degrees. He gave me a joy and an ability to enjoy what I had that I didn't have before."

DAVID ROBINSON

"God became a man and died for us, then He rose again so He can live His life through anyone who accepts Him. How can anyone not accept that when it is presented to them? I mean, it's a free gift for anyone who will receive it—eternal life."

PAUL WESTPHAL

"If you can help a young person become successful, that's going to last the rest of his life. The Bible tells us to not focus on the perishable gifts, the things that are going to vanish, but our focus needs to be on the things that are imperishable, that are going to last forever in heaven. Young people are certainly a part of that."

KEVIN JOHNSON

"God is in the forefront of my life. That defines me as a person. That defines how I play. That defines how I prepare for the game. That defines how I live off the court. And that defines how business affairs are conducted about me and around me. That's life."

A. C. GREEN

PETE MARAVICH

"Basketball was my first love, my idol, my substitute for God."

He was the skinny kid with shaggy hair and floppy socks who revolutionized the game of basketball. As a shooter, his range seemed unlimited from anywhere inside the gym. As a passer, he had no equal. Twelve-time All-Star Rick Barry said, "He could do things with a basketball I've never seen anybody do."

Pistol Pete was a legend in his own time, one of the greatest performers and players in the history of basketball and likely the most flamboyant. After becoming the only player ever to average 40 points per game for each of his three college seasons and setting the all-time college basketball scoring record at LSU, he took his act to the NBA's Atlanta Hawks, New Orleans/Utah Jazz, and Boston Celtics. He became a five-time All-Star, averaged 24 points per game over ten NBA seasons, and was inducted into the Basketball Hall of Fame in his first year of eligibility.

But more than that, Pete Maravich was a trailblazer. He single-handedly transformed the game of basketball by putting the emphasis squarely on showmanship and the showman. He was the original ringmaster of "showtime" basketball, and every arena was his three rings. He was the first athlete to make a million dollars, signing a five-year, $1.9 million contract as a rookie in 1970.

When money didn't satisfy, Pete desperately hungered for the championship ring that eluded him. Empty and frustrated, he quit the game halfway through the 1979-80 season at the age of thirty-three. Tormented by a growing void and a lack of peace, the Pistol looked for fulfillment in astrology, mysticism, Eastern religions, alcohol, survivalism, nutrition, and UFOs. Suicide was even an option.

But in 1982, Pete finally looked in the one place that would provide answers. "One night I said, 'God, can You really forgive me for what I've done? Because I've done some of the worst things in the world.' I fell off my bed and asked Christ into my life. I repented, asked for forgiveness. . . . What I've gained is a joy and a peace in my heart . . . a purpose in my life that I never had before. That emptiness, that void that was there—that was totally there—is no longer there."

Fittingly, Pistol Pete died in 1988 while playing pickup basketball. He had no championship ring, but he had peace. An autopsy determined the forty-year-old Maravich had been born without the most important artery system that supplies the heart with blood. Normal people have two systems; Pete had only one. Medical experts said that for him to have lived past twenty was extremely rare, but to play all those years with such a condition was almost impossible.

Pete Maravich was a brilliant flame that burned out much too soon. But he lasted long enough to set the basketball world on fire . . . and long enough to discover the eternal answer.

"Maravich was unbelievable.
He was ahead of his time."
MAGIC JOHNSON

"Nothing ever changed me. Not money.
Not the awards. Not popularity or fame or
adulation or material things or lust or anything
that you can talk about from a worldly
standpoint. None of that ever changed me.
The only thing that changed Pete Maravich
was Jesus Christ—totally changed me.

"If people really want to know true peace,
true joy, true happiness, money can buy you
everything but happiness. It can pay your fare
to every place but Heaven. That's what I've
found out. And I've also found out that if you
seek pleasure and happiness, you'll never,
never find it. But if you have the
wisdom to seek obedience in Jesus Christ,
happiness will find you."

PETE MARAVICH

"I wouldn't trade my position in Christ
for a thousand NBA championship rings,
for a thousand Hall of Fame rings,
or for a hundred billion dollars."

PETE MARAVICH, 1987

Heart of a Champion is a registered trademark under which virtuous sports products and programs are created and distributed. Materials include award-winning videos, television and radio programs, films, books, and Internet activities. To learn more about Heart of a Champion resources, products, or programs, call 1-800-981-9298 or visit the Web site at www.heartofachampion.com.

The Heart of a Champion Foundation is an independent, national, non-profit organization utilizing the platform of sports to build and reinforce character and ethics in young people. Blending the message and the messenger, the Heart of a Champion Foundation's winning formula teaches and models character education at the grassroots level, to mold better citizens and develop the heart of a champion in youth. For more information, visit the Web site at www.heartofachampion.org. or call (972) 497-8538.

Additional copies of this book and *Passion for the Game* and *Inspire a Dream* in the *Heart of a Champion* series are available from your local bookstore.

If you have enjoyed this book or it has impacted your life, we would like to hear from you. Please contact us at:

Honor Books
Department E
P.O. Box 55388
Tulsa, Oklahoma 74155

or by e-mail at: info@honorbooks.com

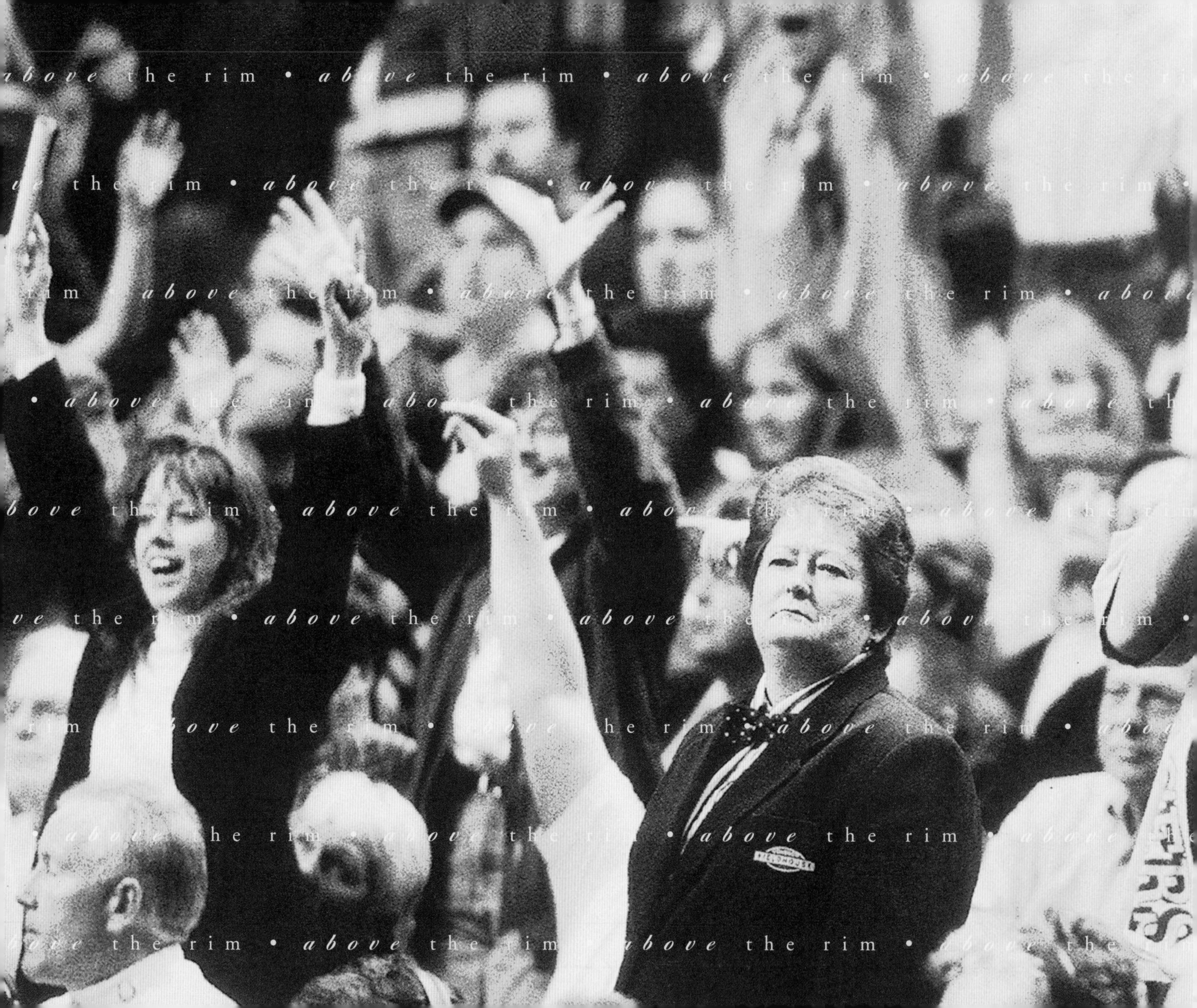
above the rim